CW01214700

IMAGES OF WA

ARMOURED WARFARE IN THE ITALIAN CAMPAIGN 1943–1945

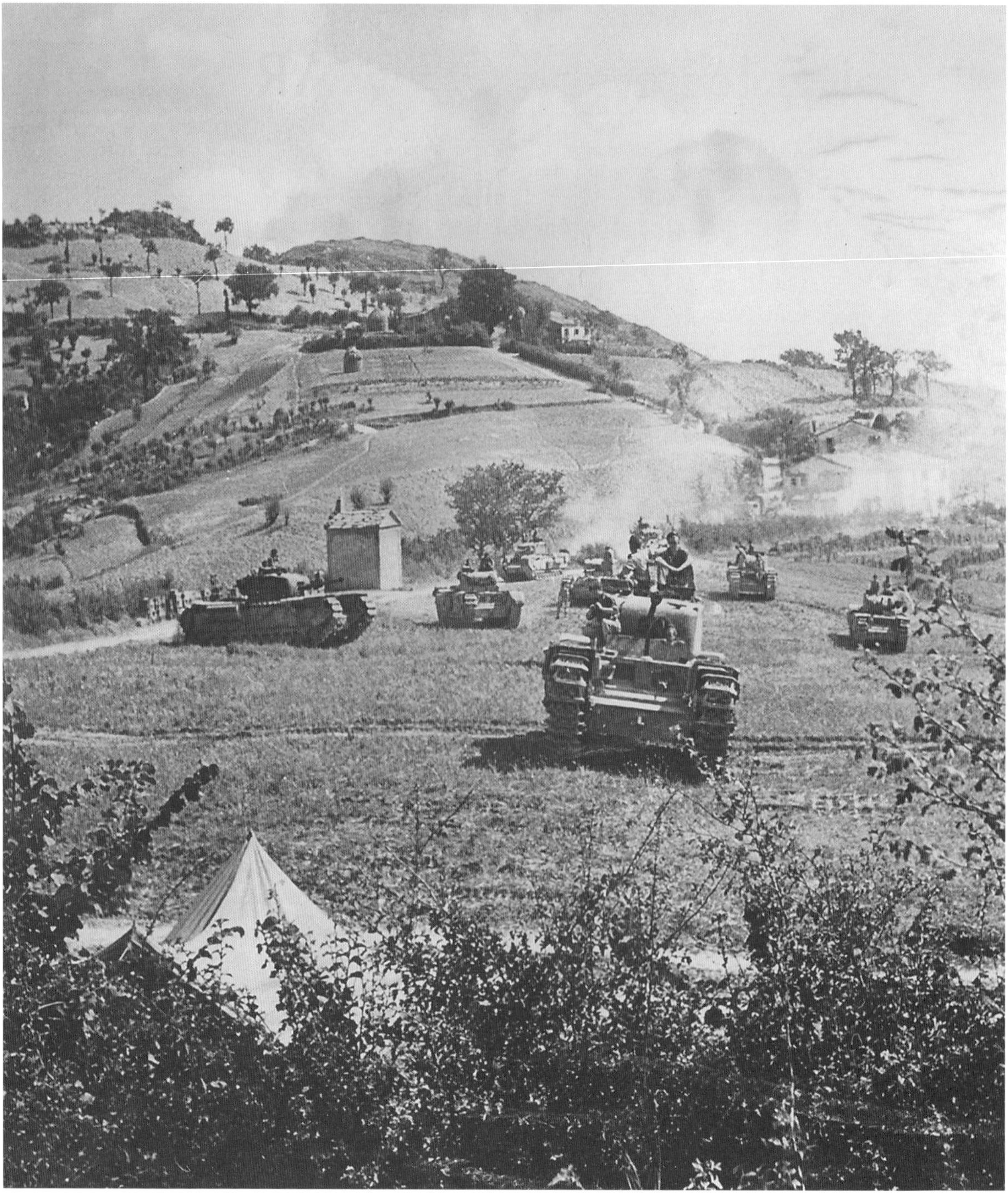

Visible are at least eight British Churchill tanks. After fighting against the Gustav Line, the British 8th Army captured Rimini and established a bridgehead over the Marno on 14 September 1944. This was subjected to fierce German counterattacks.

IMAGES OF WAR

ARMOURED WARFARE IN THE ITALIAN CAMPAIGN 1943–1945

RARE PHOTOGRAPHS FROM WARTIME ARCHIVES

Anthony Tucker-Jones

Pen & Sword
MILITARY

First published in Great Britain in 2013 by
PEN & SWORD MILITARY
an imprint of
Pen & Sword Books Ltd,
47 Church Street,
Barnsley,
South Yorkshire
S70 2AS

Copyright © Anthony Tucker-Jones, 2013
Photographs copyright © as credited, 2013

Every effort has been made to trace the copyright of all the photographs. If there are unintentional omissions, please contact the publisher in writing, who will correct all subsequent editions.

A CIP record for this book is available from the British Library.

ISBN 978 178159 247 2

The right of Anthony Tucker-Jones to be identified as Author of this Work has been asserted by him in accordance with the Copyright, Designs and Patents Act 1988.

All rights reserved. No part of this book may be reproduced or transmitted in any form or by any means, electronic or mechanical including photocopying, recording or by any information storage and retrieval system, without permission from the Publisher in writing.

Typeset by CHIC GRAPHICS

Printed and bound by CPI Group (UK) Ltd, Croydon, CR0 4YY

Pen & Sword Books Ltd incorporates the Imprints of
Pen & Sword Aviation, Pen & Sword Family History, Pen & Sword Maritime, Pen & Sword Military, Pen & Sword Discovery, Wharncliffe Local History, Wharncliffe True Crime, Wharncliffe Transport, Pen & Sword Select, Pen & Sword Military Classics, Leo Cooper, The Praetorian Press, Remember When, Seaforth Publishing and Frontline Publishing.

For a complete list of Pen & Sword titles please contact
Pen & Sword Books Limited
47 Church Street, Barnsley, South Yorkshire, S70 2AS, England
E-mail: enquiries@pen-and-sword.co.uk
Website: www.pen-and-sword.co.uk

Contents

Introduction: An Infantry War

Italian officers stood dumbfounded before the German General Westphal. He had just delivered an ultimatum: they must not resist Hitler's occupation of their country or Rome would face the wrath of the Luftwaffe. The Italian leader Benito Mussolini had first courted his Nazi counterpart in 1939 with the Pact of Steel; now the marriage was ending in an acrimonious and dramatic divorce. By the late summer of 1943 the Italians were wavering in their commitment to the Axis cause and Hitler needed to secure Italy and the Balkans against the encroaching Allies. At this point Field Marshal Albert Kesselring pulled off an audacious coup: 'Smiling Albert', with few forces to hand, browbeat, demoralised and bluffed the Italians into allowing him to occupy Rome and disarm them without even firing a shot.

In a letter to his wife dated 10 September 1943 Field Marshal Erwin Rommel, who had fought so long beside the Italians in Libya and Tunisia, said with genuine regret:

> The events in Italy have, of course, long been expected and the very situation has now arisen which we have done all we could to avoid. In the south, Italian troops are already fighting alongside the British against us. Up north, Italian troops are being disarmed for the present and sent as prisoners to Germany. What a shameful end for an army!

Before his fall from power Mussolini had wanted not additional German troops in Italy but rather German resources with which to replenish his exhausted and demoralised army. When Kesselring told Mussolini he was forming three new German divisions to help defend Italy, Mussolini remarked that they would make no difference and what he really needed was tanks and aircraft. His initial requests included 300 tanks, rising to enough equipment for 17 tank battalions and 33 self-propelled artillery battalions. The Germans scoffed at his demands.

While the campaigns fought during the Second World War in North Africa, the Eastern Front and northwest Europe were very much dominated by armoured warfare, the battles in Italy were not. The mountainous topography running the length of the Italian peninsula ensured that it was foremost an infantry war, with tanks playing a secondary supporting role. At the beginning of the campaign the mountainous terrain of southern and central Italy greatly impeded the Allied advance. When they were able to use the roads, after German demolition damage had been repaired and mines cleared, they still had to cover huge distances up zigzagging routes just to cover a few miles as the crow flies.

As well as Italy's mountains and numerous rivers, the Allies also had to overcome a number of key German defensive positions known as the Bernhardt, Gustav, Senger, Caesar, Albert, Heinrich and Gothic Lines respectively. This was a job for infantry and artillery, not tanks. On top of this, the Italian weather was an additional curse on Allied operations. For over half the year there was rain and snow, both of which resulted in mud.

Only six Allied armoured divisions fought in Italy and not all at the same time. A single US armoured division served with the multi-national US 5th Army fighting in western Italy (though independent tank battalions were assigned to support the infantry units). This was the US 1st Armored Division, affectionately known as the 'Old Ironsides'. This division was the founding unit of America's tank force during the Second World War, supplying cadres for all the other fifteen US combat armoured divisions.

However, as pointed out, the US 5th Army was a multi-national force and at various times it was strengthened by the British 6th and 7th Armoured Divisions, the South African 6th Armoured Division and the Canadian 1st Armoured Brigade. In contrast, the key armoured units with the British 8th Army fighting its way up eastern Italy were the British 1st Armoured and the Canadian 5th Armoured Divisions. The Canadians were not very happy at being equipped with the 7th Armoured Division's worn-out vehicles when the latter shipped back to Britain to take part in the Normandy landings.

Likewise, German panzer divisions were always thin on the ground in Italy. On the whole the German infantry divisions relied on the support of panzergrenadier units, which had fewer armoured fighting vehicles than the regular panzer divisions. The key armoured formation was the 26th Panzer Division, which transferred to Italy in 1943 and remained there for the rest of the war until its surrender near Bologna in May 1945. The 16th Panzer Division fought in Italy for six months between June and November 1943, seeing action at Salerno and Naples before being sent to the Eastern Front. The 24th Panzer Division was sent very briefly to northern Italy in the summer of 1943 on occupation duties.

Another panzer division that fought in both Sicily and on the Italian mainland was in fact a Luftwaffe or German Air Force unit, although in February 1943 it came under army control after General Heinz Guderian became Inspector-General

Armoured Forces. This was the volunteer Hermann Göring Panzer Division that had its origins in the elite pre-war Luftwaffe Jäeger Regiment Hermann Göring. This had become a brigade in 1942 with a paratroop and air landing training role. Early the following year it became a panzergrenadier division and finally the Fallschirm Panzer Division Hermann Göring.

The Hermann Göring Panzer Division was destroyed in Tunisia but re-formed in southern Italy and Sicily and played a key role in the Sicilian campaign in July and August 1943. Escaping to the Italian mainland following the Allied landings on Sicily, it was given the title Fallschirm Panzer Division Hermann Göring, although the Fallschirm ('Parachute') designation was purely honorary. The division was heavily involved in containing the Anzio bridgehead from January 1944 onwards until the Allied breakout. In July it was transferred to the Eastern Front.

Five panzergrenadier divisions – the 3rd, 15th, 16th SS, 29th and 90th – saw long-term action in Italy. The 15th Panzer Division, having been lost in Tunisia, was reconstituted in Sicily as the 15th Panzergrenadiers and served there and on the mainland. Most of these units started life as motorised infantry divisions and were converted in 1943. On the whole they were equipped with turretless assault guns not panzers, though the Fallschirm Panzer Division Hermann Göring included a panzer and assault gun battalion. Once the Allies had broken out of their various bridgeheads, the low-profile assault gun proved to be an ideal weapon for the Germans' defensive war in Italy.

Despite the Italian surrender on 3 September 1943, Field Marshal Kesselring seized power and stabilised the situation in Italy following the Allied landings at Salerno on the 9th. The Allied planners realised belatedly that they had lost a golden opportunity by not landing just south of Rome to pre-empt Kesselring's take-over. Not only did the Germans successfully seize most of Italy, but also the Italian-occupied zones in Albania, the Balkans, Greece and Yugoslavia, thereby securing their potentially exposed flank. Considering the German defeat at El Alamein, the subsequent Torch landings and the Germans' expulsion from North Africa and Sicily, Hitler must have been quietly pleased with how he had retrieved such a disastrous situation.

By early October Hitler had reinforced his forces in Italy with 27,000 troops that had escaped from Corsica and Sardinia. In the meantime Field Marshal Kesselring managed to keep the Allies at bay and disarm the Italian Army. He then brought the invaders to a halt 100 miles from Rome. Eight months were to pass before the Allies reached the Italian capital, and it would take another eight months before they managed to break out into the plains of northern Italy.

Four major offensives between January and May 1944 were required before the Gustav Line was eventually broken by a combined assault of the US 5th and British

8th Armies (involving British, US, French, Polish and Canadian Corps) concentrated along a 20-mile front between Monte Cassino and the western coast. The forces at Anzio did not break out of their bridgehead until late May. Even then the opportunity to cut off and destroy a large part of the German 10th Army was lost when the Anzio forces changed their direction of attack to move parallel with the coast to capture Rome. The Germans fought a highly successful and effective defensive war in Italy, which slowed down the Allied armour at every turn, until the very end of the Second World War.

Photograph Sources

The photos in this book have been sourced from the author's own extensive collection as well as various archives, including the US Army, US Signal Corps and Canadian Army Collections.

Chapter One

The Luftwaffe's Sicilian Panzers

Following the German and Italian defeat in Tunisia, the Allies turned their attentions to the Italian island of Sicily. The invasion of Sicily was not a foregone conclusion. Ideally, the Allies wanted to open a new front in western Europe, but at this stage simply did not have the resources in place to conduct a landing in northern France. Options on the table for the Allied planners included invasions of the Italian island of Sardinia or the French island of Corsica, with subsequent advances into northern Italy and southern France respectively. It was decided that an invasion of Sicily and an advance into southern Italy was the preferred option as it offered shorter and safer lines of communication with Allied forces in North Africa. Fighter cover could also be provided from Malta. Crucially this Sicilian 'right hook' alternative was intended to serve much grander goals.

Strategically, it was hoped that an attack on southern Italy would draw the Germans away from Normandy and the Eastern Front, but this led to differences of opinion among the Allies. The Americans saw the Italian campaign as a way to sap Germany's strength from more important fronts, rather than as a major effort to defeat the Axis powers in Italy. The British, on the other hand, saw a push north through Italy and into Austria and southern Germany as a way of striking at Hitler. This was an important schism because it meant that in mid-1944, at a crucial moment in the Italian campaign, the Allied armies were drained of resources to support the fighting in France.

The Germans had two armoured formations deployed on Sicily: the Luftwaffe's Hermann Göring Panzer Division commanded by General Paul Conrath and the 15th Panzergrenadier Division under General Eberhard Rodtfrom. These units could field a total of 159 tanks between them. They were reinforced by General Walter Fries' 29th Panzergrenadier Division, which began to arrive in mid-July and came under General Hans-Valentin Hube's 14th Panzer Corps.

In contrast, the Italian tank units were negligible, comprising a number of battalions of Renault R-35 tanks. The Italians had lost the bulk of their armour in the fighting in

North Africa. Very limited numbers of armoured fighting vehicles remained scattered in Albania and Greece, while the few remaining medium tanks and assault guns were gathered for the defence of mainland Italy. They were so short of tanks that when Italian officers inspected the 6th Army formations on Sicily in June they confirmed that German armour would be needed to help defend the island.

The defence of Sicily was the responsibility of the Italian 6th Army, consisting of two corps, under General Alfredo Guzzoni. However, to confuse matters the specially designated Fortress Areas around the ports came under the Italian Navy. By early July Axis forces on Sicily numbered some 200,000 Italians and 62,000 German Army and Luftwaffe personnel. The Italians were organised into four front-line infantry divisions, while the rest formed immobile coastal divisions.

For the invasion the infantry divisions of General Bernard Montgomery's British 8th Army were supported by the British 4th and 23rd Armoured Brigades and the Canadian 1st Tank Brigade. The latter, along with the Canadian 1st Infantry Division, was included at the insistence of William Lyon Mackenzie King, the Canadian prime minister. Lieutenant General George S. Patton's US 7th Army's principal supporting armoured units were the 70th and 753rd Tank Battalions and the 601st Tank Destroyer Battalion, plus elements of the 813th Tank Destroyer Battalion. Under the US Provisional Corps was the US 2nd Armored Division. The US 45th Infantry Division was also supported by a tank destroyer battalion.

Overall command and planning for Operation Husky fell to General Harold Alexander's 15th Army Group, which had the responsibility of getting Montgomery and Patton's two armies ashore on southern Sicily. General Guzzoni's 6th Army headquarters was based at Enna, in the centre of the island, while its subordinate commands consisted of General Matio Arisio's 12th Corps to the west and General Carlo Rossi's 16th Corps to the east. Reserves consisted of a single Italian division, the Hermann Göring Panzer Division and the 15th Panzergrenadiers. The poor weather meant the Italians were not anticipating any amphibious operations, so they were not on alert along the southern coast.

Operation Husky commenced on the night of 9/10 July 1943. By the evening of 10 July the assault divisions (three British, three American and one Canadian) had secured the port of Syracuse and were well established. Two days later Kesselring himself arrived to assess the situation and rapidly came to the conclusion that his troops were on their own. They needed reinforcing as quickly as possible, and in order to shorten the front line it was decided to abandon western Sicily. As a result a defensive line was established from San Stefano on the north coast via Nicosia, Agira and Cantenanuova down to Catania on the eastern coast.

As the only armoured division supporting the invasion, the US 2nd Armored was divided between two of the US 7th Army's task forces. To the left Combat

Command A (66th Armored Regiment) was with the 3rd Infantry Division coming ashore at Licata. The bulk of the division was to act as a floating reserve to support the central invasion around Gela.

In the face of counterattacks by the panzers of the Hermann Göring and Italian Livorno Divisions, plus Mobile Force E, reinforcements from the US 2nd Armored were put ashore in the shape of Combat Command B (3rd Battalion, 67th Armored Regiment). While forty panzers were overrunning the positions of the US 1st Infantry Division, the Shermans of the 2nd Armored struggled to get off the beaches. Four Shermans under Lieutenant James White finally reached the coastal highway and began to shell the Germans' flank and they eventually withdrew with the loss of sixteen tanks.

At Licata, the westernmost US beachhead, Combat Command A suffered a major reverse when the Luftwaffe hit a landing ship carrying a company of Shermans, an infantry company's vehicles and half the command's HQ equipment. Nevertheless, on 11 July the division took Naro, only to be bombed by their own air force. On 16 July 2nd Armored was placed in reserve, and then went on to take part in General Patton's attack on Palermo on the northern coast of the island. The division rolled into the city on 22 July. Once the island had been occupied, the 2nd Armored was sent to England to prepare for the Allied invasion of Normandy.

This photograph, showing a dozen M4 Shermans waiting to be loaded onto a Landing Ship Tank (LST) at La Pecherie, a French naval base in Tunisia, was taken just two days before the Allied invasion of the Italian island of Sicily. Operation Husky saw the first use of LSTs and LCTs (Landing Craft Tank) to put tanks ashore; in Algeria and Morocco the Allies had had to capture the ports first.

Following the Axis surrender in Tunisia, seventeen Tiger Is serving with the 2nd Company, Heavy Panzer Battalion 504, remained on Sicily. This 504 Tiger is making its way through a Sicilian town. Although Hitler was not keen to strengthen German forces on Sicily, he decided to reinforce the hastily reconstituted 15th Panzergrenadier Division, which had capitulated in Tunisia, with an additional division. By July the Hermann Göring Division, now equipped with the Tigers, which had been originally assigned to the 15th Panzergrenadier Division, had joined them on the island. German defenders stood at some 75,000 men with about 160 tanks.

(*Opposite*): The Italians had four field divisions with about 100 French-built light tanks and five coastal divisions totalling 275,000 men to protect Sicily. The tanks consisted mainly of tankettes and old French Renaults as well as a quantity of Fiat 3000 light tanks (essentially a copy of the Renault FT-17), armed with a 37mm gun. These were supported by a number of Semovente M41 da 90/53 self-propelled guns, as shown here. It consisted of an Italian 90/53 90mm anti-aircraft gun mounted on an M14/41 tank chassis, which went into production in 1942. It was an effective anti-tank weapon as the 53 calibre gun was more powerful than the German 88mm gun, but too few were available.

As a prelude to invasion the Allied air forces attempted to ensure that the Axis garrison was cut off and that enemy aircraft would not either hamper the landings or support their ground forces. On 5 April 1943 US B-17 Flying Fortress bombers pounded the Milo aerodrome on Sicily, catching up to eighty enemy aircraft. Many of them were German Ju 52 transport aircraft. Thirty received direct hits and many others were damaged.

This airfield at Catania on the eastern coast came under heavy attack by Liberator bombers from the US Army Air Force. The explosions straddling the main runway destroyed the administrative buildings to the left and the dispersal areas on the right.

Italian bombers, such as these Savoia-Marchetti SM 79 Sparviero (Sparrowhawks), operated from Sicily and Pantelleria in support of the Luftwaffe's air war over North Africa. By June 1943 some 1,217 Sparviero had been built, and it had become the Italian Air Force's key bomber. The Axis air forces were soon overwhelmed in the skies over Sicily.

The Italian island of Pantelleria was also subjected to ten days of Allied bombardment. This shot shows British troops from Major General Clutterbuck's British 1st Division advancing from the island's port to the airfield following Operation Corkscrew, launched on 11 June 1943. Despite being well fortified and provisioned, the 12,000-strong garrison quickly surrendered, as did those on Linosa and Lampedusa, opening the way for the invasion of Sicily.

The Sicilian port of Catania being bombed in a daylight raid just before the start of Operation Husky. Following the invasion, stalwart German defences at Catania stalled the British advance on Messina.

British airborne troops preparing to take off for Operation Ladbrooke. The 1st Air Landing Brigade was to capture the Grande Bridge over the River Anapo and then the western suburbs of Syracuse on 10 July 1943. This was designed to facilitate the advance of Major-General Berney-Ficklin's British 5th Division along the eastern coast of Sicily towards Messina.

British troops embarking for Operation Husky. Armoured support was fairly limited, comprising three British and Canadian tank brigades, a number of US tank battalions and elements of the US 2nd Armored Division.

An early production American M4A1 Sherman (identifiable by the M3-type suspension) by the name of *Eternity* comes ashore on Red Beach 2 on 10 July 1943. The German panzers and the Italian Livorno Mobile Division, the best Italian unit on the island, were ordered to counterattack the American 1st and 45th Divisions in the vicinity of Gela. The Allies took Syracuse that day and Field Marshal Kesselring decided to abandon western Sicily in order to shorten his defensive line.

(*Opposite, top*): The Husky landings were not without hazard. On 11 July the Luftwaffe hit the US Liberty Ship *Robert Rowan* off Gela with devastating results after her ammunition cargo exploded.

(*Opposite, below*): US troops examine a captured Italian self-propelled gun. The Italian Mobile Group E, consisting of over fifty light tanks, counterattacked from Niscemi towards Gela and Piano Lupo, but became tangled up with the panzers of the Hermann Göring Division. One column of twenty Italian light tanks lost two of its number to American troops with naval gunfire support before turning back.

This Luftwaffe pilot was not so lucky; his aircraft was brought down near Gela on 12 July 1943.

A British M4A2 Sherman tank of 13th Corps, 8th Army, in the streets of Francofonte among Sicilian sightseers, 13 or 14 July 1943. As the British had the more direct route, General Montgomery was determined to get to Messina before the Americans; once they got there, the Axis garrison would be trapped on the island.

Chapter Two

The Race to Messina

Despite the determined German counterattacks, the Allies drove north with little difficulty until the British 8th Army ground to a halt before Catania, just over half-way to the army's final objective: the port of Messina. Although the key strategic task had been allocated to Montgomery's 8th Army, it was the US 7th Army under the dynamic leadership of General Patton that made the real progress. By 23 July Patton's forces had cleared western Sicily and were heading eastwards along the north coast towards the prize of Messina. Their advance was assisted by a series of amphibious landings on 8, 11 and 15 August to outflank the resistance now being conducted largely by the Germans as they withdrew towards Messina.

General Hube was appointed Corps Commander on 13 July, less than two weeks before Mussolini's downfall on 25 July. German reinforcements sent to Sicily were the 1st Parachute Division and the 29th Panzergrenadier Division to add to the 15th Panzergrenadiers and the Hermann Göring Division. The 29th Panzergrenadiers were in the northern sector, the 15th in the centre and the Hermann Göring in the east. They were supported by the remnants of three Italian divisions.

The arrival of these reinforcements bolstered the German garrison to some 72,000 men with about 160 tanks, including a company of Tigers. Until the 14th Panzer Corps arrived, the new units were nominally under the command of the Italians, though in reality took their orders from General Frido von Senger und Etterlin, who was the German liaison officer with the 6th Italian Army HQ and answered to Kesselring. Hube eventually took full command of the Sicilian front in early August.

Private H.I. Tait of the 51st Highland Division witnessed the tough time that Allied tanks had on Sicily: 'One point I had particularly noted during the battle was the vulnerability of the Sherman tank, which had a much higher outline than the German tanks, and seemed to be picked off very easily. Our CO [Commanding Officer] was killed whilst in a tank conferring with the tank commander.' Private Tait also recalled the bitter fighting against the Luftwaffe's panzers for the Gerbini airfield: 'There were several counterattacks by German troops which were identified as units from the Herman Goering Division and paratroops. At about 9.00am, 21 July, there was a counterattack by German tanks supported by about a battalion strength of infantry.' During the fighting Tait was captured but managed to escape. He recalled: 'It was probably early August before our battalion went back into action. I recollect that one of our infantry companies captured a self-propelled 75mm gun by dropping into it from a tree as the gun proceeded along the road. The gun was retained.'

By late July Allied air strikes were concentrating their efforts on the panzers, especially the 15th Panzergrenadiers. They withdrew to a strongly defensive north–south line that ran through Regalbuto, conforming with the 29th Panzergrenadiers to the north and the Hermann Göring Division to the south. All three were prepared to tough it out to the end.

The Axis forces then moved to a second defensive line, anchored on Mount Etna, starting at San Fratello on the north coast and running through Troina and Aderno. The 15th Panzergrenadiers, along with the remains of an Italian infantry division, held the former. For six long days they clung on, launching twenty-four counterattacks. Once the Americans were on Mount Pellegrino, the Troina defences became untenable. The Hermann Göring Division was pushed back by 30th Corps and the 29th Panzergrenadiers' positions were turned at Santa Agata and San Fratello after the Americans landed behind them.

Catania fell on 5 August and two days later Aderno (southwest of Mount Etna) fell to the British after heavy fighting and an abrupt withdrawal by the Germans. With Aderno and Troina taken, the main defence line across northeastern Sicily was broken. On 13 August the Americans took Randazzo to the northwest of Mount Etna, some 50 miles from Messina. Efforts to trap the enemy were continually thwarted by the speed of the German withdrawal.

It was clear to Kesselring that his forces on Sicily could not hold out much longer. Hube was told to save the three German armoured units, the Hermann Göring Division and the 15th and 29th Panzergrenadiers. In Calabria the 14th Panzer Corps Mainland Corps was instructed to oversee evacuated units. German guns kept enemy fighter-bombers and warships away from the Strait of Messina so the Allies were unable to impede the German escape. Likewise, the Allies' failure to invade Calabria, the toe of Italy, thereby cutting off the Messina Straits, sealed mainland Italy's fate in becoming the next battleground.

Between 1 and 10 August some 12,000 Germans, 4,500 vehicles and 5,000 tons of equipment were successfully withdrawn to the Italian mainland. A larger-scale evacuation was conducted from 11 to 17 August. In total General Hube saved 40,000 German troops, 10,000 vehicles, 47 tanks, 94 guns and 17,000 tons of supplies, all of which were redeployed to supplement the defences of the Italian mainland. Despite this achievement, Hube lost vital equipment, including 78 tanks and armoured cars, 287 guns and 3,500 vehicles. Although the 8th Army was pressing on the Germans' heels, the honour of taking Messina fell to the US 3rd Infantry Division.

Around 62,000 Italian soldiers, 227 vehicles and 41 artillery pieces were shipped across to the mainland for the loss of 15 landing barges, 6 minesweepers and many smaller craft before the American and British armies reached Messina on 17 August. Sicily had fallen and a tremor ran through the Italian political elite in Rome. The Sicilian campaign cost the Allies almost 25,000 men, the Germans between 10,000 and 20,000, and the Italians 147,000. Crucially an entire panzer corps and its panzer and panzergrenadier divisions got away to fight another day.

The bloody fighting and resulting stalemate at Gerbina on the plains of Catania had held up Montgomery just long enough for Patton's tanks to take the laurels for winning the race to Messina. It is ironic that Patton was supposed to safeguard Montgomery's rear while Monty rushed forwards, as he had done from Alamein to Tunis.

Lieutenant General George S. Patton discusses the battle with Lieutenant Colonel Lyle Bernard, the commander of the US 30th Infantry Regiment. The British 8th Army under General Montgomery landed between Syracuse and the southeastern tip of Italy. General Patton and the US 7th Army landed in the Gulf of Gela between Licata in the west and Scoglitti in the east. The objective of both armies was Messina on the northeastern tip of the island; in the process it was hoped to trap the German and Italian forces before they could escape over the Messina Straits.

(*Above and opposite*): American GIs take a closer look at a number of knocked-out Tiger tanks. Exposed roads such as this made them vulnerable to Allied fighter-bombers. The 60-ton Tiger was soon found to be ill-suited to the rugged and unforgiving Sicilian countryside, while Italian armour was too light to offer any real resistance against American firepower.

181260

A US medic treats a casualty while poor Sicilian civilians look on. The Germans conducted a well organised fighting retreat eastwards and at no stage did this turn into a rout.

American soldiers take a rest from the fighting on Sicily in the town of Cefalu while military police in a jeep patrol the streets. The narrow streets were potential death-traps when targeted by enemy snipers.

A British early production M4A2 Sherman just north of Rammacca, which lies about 22 miles southwest of Catania and 87 miles southeast of Palermo.

(Opposite, top): This classic shot shows veterans of Montgomery's British 8th Army storming a Sicilian railway station with fixed bayonets.

(Opposite, below): Men from the 38th (Irish) Infantry Brigade conduct house clearances in Centuripe. Both photographs were taken in early August 1943.

Troops from the Canadian 1st Infantry Division enter Modica on the southern tip of Sicily.

On the whole the Italian troops on Sicily were of a poor quality and already thoroughly demoralised after their defeats in Libya and Tunisia. The Sicilian capital Palermo fell to the Allies on 22 July 1943, and by this stage some 40,000 men had been taken prisoner. Here some rather apprehensive Italians surrender to British troops.

While very few Axis tanks escaped over the Messina Straits, tens of thousands of troops crossed largely unmolested. This photo shows Messina's railyards under air attack. The air defences here were particularly strong.

Canadian tanks of the Regiment de Trois-Rivieres entering the ruins of Regalbuto, 4 August 1943.

The final resting place for another knocked-out Tiger in the Sicilian countryside. The Germans left behind seventy-eight tanks and armoured cars following the evacuation, but 55,000 troops escaped.

Chapter Three

Kesselring's Italian Coup

After the surrender of the Axis forces in Tunisia, the writing was on the wall for Mussolini, and his fate was sealed when Allied troops assaulted Italian soil with the invasion of Sicily. The fighting on the island triggered a political crisis in metropolitan Italy. Fifteen days after the invasion Mussolini was arrested in Rome and the new government under General Badoglio began to secretly negotiate with the Allies. Hitler was furious, and did not trust Badoglio's claims that Italy would remain loyal to the German cause. General Jodl, Hitler's Chief of Operations, urged caution but the Fuhrer knew the situation called for decisive action by his panzers before his southern flank became unhinged.

Just two days after Mussolini's fall, Hitler convened an emergency conference and presented four military options for dealing with Italy if she should abandon the Axis cause. The first, Operation Eiche (Oak), envisaged a maritime or airborne rescue mission to secure Mussolini's release; the second, Operation Student, was more ambitious and called for the seizure of Rome in order to reinstate Mussolini; the third, Operation Schwarz (Black), proposed the total occupation of Italy and the fourth, Operation Achse (Axis), planned for the capture or destruction of the Italian fleet. The last two were to be combined under the codename Axis.

By late July Hitler, fearing the worst, drafted War Directive 49 outlining the occupation of Italy and all her overseas possessions. The directive was never issued, but on 31 July a series of separate orders were sent out informing commanders of what they should do if the Italians dropped out of the war. Although Hitler was dissuaded from putting the 3rd Panzergrenadiers on the streets of Rome, he swiftly secured the Alpine passes between Germany and Italy, and between Italy and France. Eight divisions were assembled from France and southern Germany as Army Group B, ready to rescue those German forces in Italy.

Had the Italians acted decisively they could have sealed the Alpine bridges and tunnels and cut off the Wehrmacht already in Italy. The Italians had prepared the

Brenner Pass for demolition, and had they blown the vital rail link it would have been out of action for at least six months. However, changing sides took time and Badoglio had to establish contact with the Allies and agree terms for an armistice before he could act against his former comrades in arms. Six precious weeks were to be wasted, leaving Italy vulnerable to Hitler's counterstroke.

According to the German Intelligence Bureau established to monitor Italian troop movements in the north, the Italian Army was suffering a severe ammunition shortage. Field Marshal Rommel, placed in command of securing Italy, was not surprised: he already had a low opinion of Italian industry after his experience with the ill-resourced Italian forces in North Africa.

Belatedly the Italians moved the Alpine, Julia and Trentina Divisions to the Brenner. The road to the Italian naval base at La Spezia was also blocked. On 9 August Rommel wrote to his wife: 'The situation with these unreliable Italians is extremely unpleasant. To our faces they protest their truest loyalty to the common cause, and yet they create all kinds of difficulties for us and at the back of it all seem to be negotiating.' The Germans also became alarmed by the Italian withdrawal of their occupation forces from southern France, and the movement of two Italian divisions from southern Italy to the north.

'General Feuerstein reports that a critical situation developed on the Brenner about midday yesterday [1/8/43],' recorded Rommel in his diary, 'when the Italians tried to hold up the advance of 44th Infantry Division. General Gloria had given orders for fire to be opened if 44th Division attempted to continue its march.' Fortunately the Italian troops on the ground chose not to obey the order and instead withdrew. The Italians concentrated 60,000 men in the Verona–Bolzano area but, in the face of the tanks of the 1st SS Panzer Division, which crossed the Brenner Pass on 3 August, chose not to deploy them. The panzers rolled over the frontier alert to possible resistance, but in the event the only casualties were two Tiger tanks, which did not like the concrete roads: one overturned and another caught fire. In truth, the 1st SS Panzer Division was a bit disorganised as all its armour had been left in Russia and it had to re-equip en route.

Rather than defend the whole of Italy, the Germans drew up plans for a defensive line in the Apennines well to the north of Rome. During August the 1st SS and 25th Panzer Divisions and five infantry divisions crossed the frontier. In central Italy the German 10th Army was activated; it was able to call on five divisions and another two near Rome. Up until the end of the Sicilian campaign, and the successful escape of four German divisions, Hitler only had two divisions covering the whole of southern Italy. The Italians were not pleased about the presence of these German troops and Kesselring's Chief of Staff, General Siegfried Westphal, spent a great deal of time trying to smooth ruffled feathers.

On 15 August Rommel travelled to Bologna to discuss the situation with General Roatta, Chief of Staff of the Italian Army. To his alarm, German intelligence indicated that the Italians intended to either poison him or have him arrested; in response he took with him German panzergrenadiers to secure the conference building beforehand. Roatta claimed the withdrawal of Italian troops from southern France was to help fight the British, and that the Alpine division from southern Italy had moved simply north to resume garrison duties. He confirmed that a second division had moved also north, to secure the railways from sabotage. Roatta dismissed any ideas that these refitting formations were in any way a threat to German interests.

Roatta reiterated that the defence of Italian soil against the Allies must be left to the Italian Army, though the Germans could take over air defence. He also tried to get rid of the powerful 1st SS Panzer Division by suggesting it be sent to Sardinia; he also suggested that other German forces should be moved into southern Italy. The meeting broke up without agreement and the following day Italian representatives offering Italy's unconditional surrender approached the British Ambassador in Madrid.

After securing Sicily in August, the Allies invaded mainland Italy at Reggio, Salerno and Taranto at the beginning of the following month. The Italians lost an estimated 2,000 dead, 5,000 wounded and 137,000 captured on Sicily, along with all their tanks. This final military disaster was a blow from which the Italian Army would not recover. By September the Italian Army had twenty-one divisions in mainland Italy, although half of these were of poor quality, plus four in Sardinia and another thirty-six overseas. To fend off a German takeover of northern and central Italy, the Italian Army had eight infantry divisions and two motorised/armoured divisions, supported by another eight (weak) infantry divisions. Against these forces the Germans could field about sixteen highly experienced divisions.

If the Allied invasion fleet gathered off Naples on 8 September had sailed north and put its forces ashore near the Italian capital, the Italian Army would probably have used its remaining tanks against the Germans and Hitler would have abandoned Kesselring and his eight divisions. Instead, fate took a cruel turn and the American 5th Army landed not near Rome but at Salerno, south of Naples. Kesselring's HQ at Frascati, near Rome, lost all communication with the outside world on the 8th after an American air raid killed nearly a hundred of his staff.

Following the Italian armistice with the Allies on 9 September, Hitler issued the codeword Achse (Axis). When the Germans learned of the armistice through a BBC broadcast, Kesselring was alerted. For a day or two the fate of those German forces in central and southern Italy hung in the balance. A tense stand-off took place between two German divisions and five Italian divisions equipped with tanks near the Italian capital. During 1943 the Italian Army had received an updated version of their medium tank, designated the M15/42. By September just over eighty had been delivered and these were deployed around Rome.

General Westphal, trying to reach General Roatta at Monte Rotondo, found himself obstructed by troops from the Italian Grenadier Division. Fearing something was wrong, Westphal insisted on seeing Roatta, and upon his arrival the Italian general informed him that Italy had signed an armistice with the Allies. Returning to Frascati, Westphal acted quickly and with more aggression than Kesselring would have liked. He called a conference with the General Staff of General Carboni's Italian Corps, which was responsible for Rome.

Once the Italian officers were gathered, Westphal expressed his regret that they were no longer comrades in arms (he had served alongside them in North Africa). He said they had two options: either to lay down their arms or to suffer Stuka dive-bomber attacks. In support of this threat, Field Marshal von Richthofen had eighty fighter aircraft at his disposal in Italy. The next day an Italian officer arrived and signed the surrender order for the Carboni Corps. Kesselring and Westphal heaved a sign of relief that their coup would be bloodless. The Wehrmacht took possession of two-thirds of Italy, including the industrial north, whose factories were soon put to work churning out arms for the German war effort.

Hitler's next move was to 'rescue' Mussolini, and for this job he called on SS-Sturmbannfuhrer Otto Skorzeny. On 12 September Mussolini was snatched from the Hotel Albergo-Rifugo 100 miles from Rome. A German glider landed in the hotel grounds and disgorged a number of Waffen-SS commandos and an Italian general. The carabinieri guarding Mussolini were unsure what to do; some simply fled, while the others faced the quandary of whether to open fire on an Italian general, or indeed their former leader. At the behest of Skorzeny and Mussolini, they decided to lay down their arms.

Skorzeny hurried the former dictator to a small plane and he was flown to Vienna via Rome. A few days later he arrived at Rastenburg to meet his saviour. While Mussolini was full of gratitude, Hitler was displeased to find his one-time ally was less than enthusiastic about his plans to revive fascism in northern Italy. The disillusioned Mussolini found himself the puppet ruler of his German-occupied homeland, the so-called Repubblica Sociale Italiana (RSI). In reality, all he wanted to do was spend time with his mistress while Italy went to ruin.

The fighting on Sicily triggered a political crisis in metropolitan Italy. Fifteen days after the invasion Mussolini was arrested in Rome and the new government under General Badoglio began to negotiate with the Allies. Hitler was furious and did not believe Badoglio's claims that Italy would remain loyal to the German cause. General Jodl, Hitler's Chief of Operations, urged caution, but the Fuhrer knew the situation called for decisive action before Germany's southern flank became unhinged.

In the late summer of 1943 Field Marshal 'Smiling Albert' Kesselring pulled off an audacious coup in Italy: with few forces to hand, he browbeat, demoralised and bluffed the Italians into allowing him to occupy Rome and disarm them without even firing a shot. Kesselring (seen inspecting his troops) was to prove a very tough adversary in Italy.

The panzers rolled over the Italian border in early August 1943 and the Italian Army chose not to resist. The only casualties were two Tiger tanks lost to mechanical problems. The 1st SS Panzer, 25th Panzer and 64th Infantry Divisions crossed the Brenner Pass unhindered, despite the presence of some 60,000 Italian troops.

(*Above*): German security units spearheaded by armoured cars such as this Sd Kfz 232 spread out across northern Italy to pre-empt the country's defection to the Allies. Production of this type of armoured car ceased in September 1942 in favour of the 234 series armed with a 75mm anti-tank gun.

(*Opposite*): Although a stand-off took place near Rome between two German divisions and five Italian divisions equipped with tanks, the Italians chose not to fight. As a result, all their heavy equipment such as these Semovente assault guns fell into German hands and were despatched south to fight the Allies.

A similar fate befell these Italian Semovente M41 da 90/53 self-propelled guns. The open fighting compartment left the crew vulnerable but such weapons provided useful stopgaps.

This L3 tankette was requisitioned by the 7th SS Mountain Division.

The Germans also recycled captured British equipment in Italy, such as this carrier. Having been rearmed with an MG 42 machine gun, it was used to provide transport for a German Panzerfaust team.

(*Above*): British infantry hurrying past two knocked-out Panzer Mk IVs. Although the Allied landings in southern Italy were successful, the panzers swiftly secured northern Italy for Hitler's war effort.

(*Opposite*): Allied Shermans pushing north after the landings on mainland Italy. The country's geography was ill-suited for offensive tank warfare and was much better suited to the needs of the defenders.

Hitler's latest Panzer, the Mk V, known as the Panther, did not arrive in Italy until the spring of 1944 in time to help counter Operation Diadem. This was the first of three different models known as the Panzerkampfwagen V Ausf D, which were initially issued to the 1st SS and 2nd SS Panzer Divisions on the Eastern Front.

Chapter Four

Battle of the Bridgeheads

Having secured Sicily, the Allies invaded mainland Italy. The main assault, under the codename Operation Avalanche, took place on the western coast at Salerno, with two subsidiary operations taking place in Calabria and Taranto. The Salerno invasion force consisted of 100,000 British troops and 69,000 Americans, with some 20,000 vehicles borne by an armada of 450 vessels. The key armoured unit was the British 7th Armoured Division, while supporting forces also included the Royal Scots Greys and the 40th Royal Tank Regiment. The US 5th Army's reserves included the US 1st Armored Division. Under Operation Baytown the Canadian 1st Armoured Division came ashore at Reggio di Calabria, supporting the British 8th Corps.

Following the Axis surrender in Tunisia, the British 7th Armoured Division was withdrawn to Tripolitania to refit. It did not participate in Operation Husky, and instead trained for a role in the amphibious assault on mainland Italy. The battle-hardened veterans of 22 Armoured Brigade were brought back up to strength and issued with new vehicles and equipment. They cast off most of their British tanks and were equipped almost exclusively with the M4 Sherman. Their divisional armoured car regiment had Daimler and Dingo armoured cars supplemented with White scout cars.

To beef up the division's anti-tank capabilities, the Jeep troop was replaced by a self-propelled gun troop equipped with two 75mm guns mounted in White half-tracks to give immediate fire support. At the same time the 5th Royal Horse Artillery was issued with the Priest 105mm self-propelled gun to work in conjunction with the armoured brigade's tanks. In light of the terrain in Italy, the engineers were trained to deploy new Bailey bridges and tank-mounted scissor bridges in order to keep the division moving.

Field Marshal Rommel had taken charge of Army Group B in mid-August with responsibility for all German forces in Italy as far as Pisa. Field Marshal Kesselring and Army Command South remained in charge in southern Italy. The newly formed German 10th Army under General Heinrich von Vietinghoff was activated on 22 August with the task of fending off an Allied invasion. This army controlled the 14th

Panzer Corps (Hermann Göring Panzer, 15th Panzergrenadier and 16th Panzer Divisions) and the 76th Panzer Corps (26th Panzer and 29th Panzergrenadier Divisions). Most notably, the 16th Panzer Division was deployed above the Salerno plain.

Following Operation Baytown on 3 September 1943, Kesselring rightly deduced that the Calabria landings were not the main Allied effort and concluded that Salerno or Rome would be their main point of attack. He withdrew General Traugott Herr's 76th Panzer Corps, leaving just a regiment of panzergrenadiers to hold the toe of Italy in the face of the British 8th Army.

On 9 September Operation Slapstick seized Taranto unopposed, followed by Bari and Brindisi. The assault at Salerno also commenced that day, although the Allies soon found elements of the 16th Panzer, Hermann Göring Panzer and 15th and 29th Panzergrenadier Divisions bearing down on them. Private J.C. Jones from the US 36th Infantry Division remembered,

> Beyond the beaches in front of the 141st [Regiment], the relatively flat terrain was now invaded by five Mark IV (medium) tanks. The German armour rolled over the American troops who had taken cover in the irrigation ditches, firing continual machine-gun bursts into the prone men as they rumbled by. A platoon of B Company, led by Staff Sgt James A. Whitaker of Brownwood, Texas, was caught by these tanks.

By 13 September all German reinforcements were in position, including units from the 3rd Panzergrenadier Division, which had been north of Rome. That day they launched a counteroffensive, which was halted by naval gunfire and artillery. Two days later the 16th Panzer and 29th Panzergrenadier Divisions went over to the defensive, while the Hermann Göring Division achieved some success east of Salerno. On 15 September, carrying infantry on their backs, the Shermans of the 40th Royal Tank Regiment departed Salerno en route for Naples.

When the 7th Armoured Division arrived in Italy on 15 September in support of the US 5th Army, its units were soon confronted with poor roads, mountains and impassable rivers. They acted as the follow-up division supporting the British 46th and 56th Infantry Divisions at Salerno. By 16 September the British and American bridgeheads had linked up, with the US 5th Army pushing up the west coast and the British 8th Army advancing along the east coast. The 7th Armoured Division's first real success was the taking of Scafati on the Sarno river. Having secured the town's road bridge intact, divisional engineers then erected a Bailey bridge next to it. Forward elements of the 7th Armoured Division entered Naples on 1 October.

Once beyond Naples, the armour was able to fan out. By 5 October the 7th

Armoured's tanks had reached the Volturno river near Capua. The Germans, however, had blown all the bridges and were firmly dug in on the far bank. On 12 October the 7th Armoured Division, acting in support of an infantry assault, launched a diversionary crossing to keep the Germans preoccupied. The tanks managed to ford the river and help turn the enemy's defences. The Germans, though, simply withdrew to their next defence line along the Garigliano river.

In light of the Allies' superior firepower, both the 76th and 14th Panzer Corps had little option but to break off the battle. Nonetheless, the armoured formations of the 10th Army had come very close to overcoming the Salerno bridgehead. The initial conduct of the 16th Panzer Division and the Germans' ability to redeploy their forces more quickly than the Allies could reinforce almost tipped the battle in their favour.

The whole of southern Italy was in Allied hands by early October, and they now faced a whole series of German defensive lines. These would buy the Germans time while they constructed the 'Winter Line' south of Rome. In November the 7th Armoured Division was pulled back behind Monte Massico as it had been earmarked to take part in the coming Allied invasion of Normandy. The men handed over all their Sherman tanks and equipment to the Canadian 5th Armoured Division and made their way to Naples ready to be shipped back to England. There they re-equipped with British-built Cromwell tanks – with dire consequences (see *Images of War: Armoured Warfare in the Battle for Normandy*).

By early November Hitler had dispatched Rommel to oversee the defence of northern France and Kesselring was left in charge in Italy with instructions to deny Rome to the Allies for as long as possible. It took the Allies until mid-January 1944 to force their way through the Volturno, Barbara and Bernhardt Lines to reach the Gustav Line – the centrepiece of the Winter Line.

The Allies launched their offensive in the south on 12 January 1944, with General Juin's French Expeditionary Corps assaulting Cassino and the British 10th Corps attempting to exploit previous gains on the Garigliano river. Both assaults failed to break through the German Gustav Line, although limited progress was made.

A week later the US 2nd Corps attacked from the centre of General Mark Clark's US 5th Army, attempting to cross the Rapido river, but after just two days the Americans were forced to call a halt. The breakthrough of the Gustav Line – the lynch-pin of the Allied plan, of which Operation Shingle (the Anzio landing) was a part – had bogged down. This lack of success at Cassino indicated there would be no progress towards Rome during March.

Operation Shingle, launched on 22 January 1944, was an amphibious attack in the area of Anzio and Nettuno, designed to turn the German flank and compromise their defences. Some 36,000 troops and 3,200 vehicles poured ashore. British forces hitting 'Peter Beach' were backed by the 46th Royal Tank Regiment, while the American troops coming ashore on 'X-Ray Beach' had armoured support from the 751st Tank Battalion and 601st Tank Destroyer Battalion. Six days earlier the US 5th Army had struck the Gustav Line at Monte Cassino; although it failed to achieve a breakthrough, it drew German reinforcements in the form of the 29th and 90th Panzergrenadier Divisions away from Rome.

At Anzio the Allies soon found their way blocked by the Hermann Göring Panzer Division and a battle group from the 4th Parachute Division, which were holding the roads from Anzio to the Alban Hills via Campoleone and Cisterna. Just two days after the landings the Germans had over 40,000 troops in the area, with the 4th Parachute Division to the west, the 3rd Panzergrenadiers in front of the Alban Hills and the Hermann Göring Division to the east. The invasion forces were hemmed in by elements of the 26th Panzer and Hermann Göring Divisions, as well as the 3rd and 16th SS Panzergrenadier Divisions with about 220 panzers. In two weeks of fighting the Anglo-American forces suffered almost 7,000 casualties.

By early February some 76,000 troops were facing 100,000 Germans under the control of the 14th Army and the 76th Panzer Corps and 1st Parachute Corps. The Germans launched a counterattack on 3 February and again on 16 February, with both sides fighting each other to a standstill. All the time the Allied forces at Anzio remained bottled up, they were tying up the valuable shipping that was keeping them resupplied. Due to the lack of progress, Lieutenant General Lucian Truscott replaced General Lucas as the commander at Anzio. Once again the panzers had triumphed.

Lieutenant General Mark W. Clark, commander of the US 5th Army, onboard the USS *Ancon* for the Salerno landings on 12 September 1943. This heralded the Allies' attack on mainland Italy following their success in Sicily.

British motor transport and anti-aircraft guns coming ashore from LST 383 during the Salerno landings. Operation Avalanche involved almost 170,000 Allied troops and some 20,000 vehicles; initially they met minimal enemy resistance.

314
T83025

American artillery and trucks being landed at Salerno. The military policeman on the right is ducking away from the blast of an incoming German 88mm round.

(*Opposite*): A column of British Carriers off-loaded from LST 314; note the array of anti-aircraft guns on the prow of the vessel. The British 7th Armoured Division came ashore on 15 September 1943, six days after the landings commenced.

Forward elements of the British 7th Armoured Division liberated Naples on 1 October 1943. This shot shows British 17-pounder anti-tank guns making their way through the narrow streets of Scafati. The whole of southern Italy was in Allied hands by early October.

(*Opposite, top*): Once beyond Naples, the Allied armour began to fan out. By 5 October 1943 the 7th Armoured Division had reached the Volturno river near Capua. This river was one of the major barriers to the advance on Rome. This photograph shows British infantry supported by M4 Sherman tanks moving up towards the Volturno, where they launched a diversionary crossing on the 12th.

(*Opposite, below*): British infantry clearing the village of Sparanise, northwest of Capua, on 23 October 1943, after several days of fighting.

PANETTERIA

American engineers from the US 5th Army overseeing a pontoon bridge across the Volturno. On 13 October 1943, under the cover of darkness, lightly equipped infantry made a night crossing in assault boats. Sherman tanks were also landed from LSTs on the northern mouth of the river. Ammunition for the anti-tank guns and the tanks was then ferried over by amphibious craft manned by American crews.

(*Opposite, top*): British infantry crossing a pontoon bridge over the Volturno. It is not clear if this is the same bridge as in the previous image. A well concealed anti-aircraft gun mounted on a pontoon is just visible to the right by the far bank.

(*Opposite, below*): British infantry serving with the US 5th Army trudging through the mud in the Volturno bridgehead. In the meantime the Germans withdrew to their next defensive line along the Garigliano river.

British and American vehicles serving with 5th Army on the streets of Majori in October 1943. They include the six guns of a British Bofors anti-aircraft battery passing up the road. Visible in the foreground are General Motors Corporation 6x6 lorries, and in the background Chevrolet 4x4 lorries.

Allied bombers striking German positions at Lanciano in support of the British 8th Army's bridgeheads north of the Sangro river. Note that the roads are clear of vehicles.

Another shot of the attacks on Lanciano. The inky clouds above the bombers are bursts of flak.

The following month bombers of the South African Air Force successfully destroyed the vital German ammunition dump at Alfadena. In the face of Allied air superiority, the Germans struggled to keep their units in Italy resupplied.

In an effort to break the deadlock in Italy and turn the German defences, it was decided to make an amphibious left hook at Anzio in January 1944 with Operation Shingle. These men are from the US 3rd Ranger Battalion; nearly all of them would be killed or captured at Cisterna.

(Opposite, top): The Anzio landing was virtually unopposed, as this Sherman advancing on X-Ray Beach on 22 January clearly shows. However, it was not long before the Allies were hemmed in by battle-hardened panzer and panzergrenadier divisions.

(Opposite, below): This GI is taking a closer look at the remains of a German Marder III self-propelled gun. Panzerjäger detachments of both the panzer and infantry divisions were issued with these guns from May 1943.

Another German self-propelled gun mounted on the same chassis. Known as the Grille, it was armed with a 150mm howitzer and served with the heavy infantry assault companies of the panzergrenadier regiments in Italy. This one was photographed firing from a position between the ruins of Carroceto near Aprilia on 26 February 1944. Behind it is a knocked-out Sherman and an Sd Kfz 251 half-track.

German paratroops of the Fallschirm Hermann Göring Panzer Division passing an immobilised Elefant during a counterattack on the Anzio bridgehead on 17 February 1944. These tank destroyers were issued to Heavy Panzerjäger Battalion 653, and elements of this unit were shipped to Italy. The Elefants saw action at Nettuno, Anzio and Cisterna, but in April 1944 part of the battalion was sent back to the Eastern Front.

An abandoned Elefant captured by the Allies. In September 1943, after a poor showing on the Eastern Front, the Germans withdrew the Ferdinand for modifications, which included the installation of a much-needed ball-mounted machine gun in the front of the hull, a modified StuG III commander's cupola to help with visibility and a coat of Zimmerit anti-magnetic paste. These modest improvements pushed its weight up from 65 to 70 tons. The modernised version of the Ferdinand was dubbed the Elefant, and this new name became official by order of Hitler himself on 1 May 1944. Their sheer weight meant that they were too heavy for most Italian roads and bridges, and soon became stranded.

An American bazooka team engaging German targets. This was the US Army's standard infantry anti-tank weapon in Italy.

A bogged-down StuG III assault gun, photographed in early January 1944. Note the piles of spare road wheels stacked on the back. The Sturmgeschütz detachments of the Hermann Göring Panzer Division were issued with the Ausf F, though the Ausf G seen here was much more common.

(Opposite, top): This abandoned Panzer Mk IV Ausf H was found hiding in a haystack near Szee. Between April 1943 and July 1944 the Germans produced 3,774 examples of the Ausf H, making it the most numerous Panzer IV model.

(Opposite, below): When the Panzer Mk V Ausf A Panther was first introduced, it saw service in Italy but it did not arrive there until the late spring of 1944.

725

LST 77 off-loading M4A2 Sherman tanks at Anzio, Italy, May 1944. Note the small capsized barge in the background.

Chapter Five

Mussolini's Shanghaied Panzers

The Italian Army and its tanks were much maligned during the Second World War, particularly after their lacklustre performance in North Africa and on the Eastern Front. The irony is that Italian tanks, or more specifically assault guns, only came into their own after the Germans confiscated them and used them to resist the Allies in Italy. The Italians' best armoured fighting vehicles were a series of assault guns based on the medium tank chassis that appeared from 1941 onwards.

These assault guns were well suited to the Wehrmacht's defensive battles fought to prevent the Allies progressing up the Italian peninsula. The Germans seized almost 200 Semoventes, a number that was to double with continued production; some of these were issued to the 26th Panzer and 336th Infantry Divisions serving in Italy. Overall Italian assault guns equipped two panzer, three panzergrenadier and six infantry divisions, plus one mountain division, fighting in Italy and the Balkans. The Germans also confiscated a small number of M13/40 and M14/41 medium tanks and almost a hundred M15/42s, some of which were issued to two SS Sturmgeschutz detachments, Panzer Battalion Adria and Mussolini's puppet state Repubblica Sociale Italiana's (RSI) armoured units.

In May 1943 thirty-six panzers were supplied to Italy to form a new crack division named the 'Mussolini' (1st) Armoured Division, or the 'Leonessa' Armoured Group. Raised from the Italian fascist militia, this unit was only of brigade strength, equipped with twelve Pz Kpfw IV Ausf Hs, twelve Pz Kpfw III Ausf Ns and twelve StuG III Ausf Gs. After the armistice the unit was disbanded and the panzers confiscated.

The Italians had recognised the shortcomings of their tank design from the very start of the war, but were never able to rectify the situation. They soon found the L3 tankette was not suitable for modern tank warfare and the M11/39 medium tank was poorly designed. At the first opportunity the latter (which suffered mechanical problems and had armour that was too thin and a gun that lacked punch) had been replaced with the much better M13/40 and the slightly improved M14/41. Indeed these models, despite heavy losses, remained the standard Italian medium tanks throughout the war. The improved M15/42 medium tank had an increased calibre gun and a more powerful engine, but was only produced in very limited numbers in early 1943. As is transpired, it appeared just in time to fall into German hands.

The Italian armistice with the Allies on 9 September 1943 resulted in Hitler issuing the codeword 'Axis', alerting German forces in Italy to take control. The Italian Army had received the new M15/42 and by September just over eighty had been delivered to those units deployed around Rome, thereby obstructing German plans. Resistance, though, was short-lived. The Italian Army handed over all its equipment to the Wehrmacht, except in Albania, where an Italian division joined the partisans. Demoralised Italian troops were disarmed almost without firing a shot and the Germans confiscated all their weapon stocks. It was a shameful way to treat a former ally.

Not only did the Germans confiscate all the Italian Army's armour, but they forced the Italians to continue manufacturing the M15/42 and P26/40 tanks, as well as the 75/18, 105/25 and 75/46 Semovente self-propelled guns for their own use. Following the successful completion of Operation Axis, Hitler was informed that the newly designed Italian P26/40 had the best armour of any captured tank. He authorised the construction of 150 of them to equip four regiments, but problems with the engines meant only sixty were ever supplied. Overall, through seizures from the Italian Army and continuing limited production, the Wehrmacht gained almost a thousand much-needed tanks, assault guns and armoured cars at a very critical moment in the war.

Once Italy's industries were firmly under German control, they were forced to produce vehicles for the Wehrmacht whether they liked it or not. The Germans not only kept up a limited production of Italian tanks but also motor vehicles such as Alfa Romeo, Fiat and Spa trucks. Alfa Romeo, Bianchi, Isotta-Fraschini, Lancia and OM had manufactured trucks for the Italian Army, and both the German and British forces in North Africa had made considerable use of them.

Fiat-Ansaldo was the main Italian tracked and wheeled armoured vehicle manufacturer. The Germans quickly took over the Fiat works in Turin and its subsidiary OM in Milan, along with Alfa Romeo, Bianchi, Breda, Isotta-Fraschini and Pavesi, also all in Milan. The Germans also put into production the Breda 61 semi-track artillery tractor, essentially an Italian copy of the German Sd Kfz 7 half-track. Several hundred were built in 1943–44 mainly for the Wehrmacht. Lancia also built 250 Lince scout cars, based on the British Daimler scout car, in 1944 for Italian paramilitary and police forces.

Despite this enforced production Fiat was not greatly cooperative and in Turin there were strikes, sabotage and other forms of collective resistance. By the beginning of 1944 the Germans' exasperated response was to order all Fiat production equipment shipped to Germany; the resulting general strike right across northern Italy ensured that Fiat stayed put. Everything ground to a halt and during the first three months of 1945 Fiat only produced ten trucks a day.

After being rescued from house arrest, the disillusioned Mussolini found himself the puppet ruler of his German-occupied homeland, the so-called Repubblica Sociale Italiana (RSI). Italy fell into a state of civil war as some Italian units sided with the Allies in the south while others continued to fight for Mussolini and his Nazi masters in the north.

Hitler did not allow the RSI's armed forces to have any significant numbers of tanks, for obvious reasons. The Republican Army numbered 400,000 men and, along with the 150,000-strong Guardia Nazionale Repubblicana (GNR), it was on the whole only ever used to fight Italian resistance forces operating in northern Italy. Just two armoured groups – 'Leoncello' and 'San Giusto' – equipped with some M13/40 and M14/41 medium tanks supported the four divisions of the RSI Army, while the GNR Combattente had a single armoured battalion.

The British and American armies had ample experience of fighting Italian armour during the campaigns in North Africa, but imagine their surprise when they came up against Italian tanks and assault guns on the Italian mainland sporting German markings and manned by panzertruppen. In fending off Operation Diadem in May 1944 the Germans lost 150 tanks and 300 self-propelled guns – half the available armour in Italy. These losses show just what a valuable contribution the Italian armour played in the German war effort in Italy. By the end of December 1944 there were still 161 Italian tanks and assault guns serving German units in Italy.

The Italians had manufactured almost 800 M13/40s and about 900 of the slightly improved M14/41s by September 1943; following the occupation of Italy the Germans managed to build only another twenty-two M13s and a single M14. These M13/40s, pictured in North Africa, were captured by the Allies.

(Opposite, top): By the end of December 1944 there were just sixty-eight M13/40s (seen here), M14/41s and M15/42s still serving the Germans in Italy.

(Opposite, below): The M15/42 medium tank featured slightly heavier frontal armour, a longer gun and a new, more powerful motor than the earlier models. Only eighty-two had been delivered to the Italian Army before September 1943 and these were used for the defence of Rome. Another thirty had just been finished so the Germans confiscated a total of ninety-two. The M15 is distinguishable from the M13 and M14 by the location of the access door on the right-hand side of the superstructure, rather than the left.

(*Above and opposite*): The Germans seized almost 200 Semoventes, a number that was to double with continued production. Italian assault guns equipped two panzer, three panzergrenadier, six infantry and one mountain divisions fighting in Italy and the Balkans.

FOTOGRAFI
6225

The Italian Semovente M40/M41 was redesignated the StuG M40 und M41 mit 75/18 850(i) in German service and proved an ideal weapon for the defensive battles fought in Italy.

Another Semovente formerly in German service.

This Semovente DA 75/34 was captured in Italy, having been press-ganged into service with the Germans as the Sturmgeschütz M42. It is a source of some amusement for a British tank crew.

An abandoned Semovente DA 105/25 serving with the German forces as the Sturmgeschütz M43 mit 105/25 853(i). This one appears to have come off the road, got stuck in a ditch and broken down. It was probably abandoned but there is no sign that its crew set it alight.

Italian L.3/33 and L.3/35 tankettes with their new masters. As the Italians had built over 2,000 of these vehicles there were still considerable numbers available after the Germans had taken over.

(*Opposite, top*): British troops on a captured Panzerkampfwagen P40 737(i), formerly the Italian P26/40. The Italians had been developing a heavy tank since 1940 and by 1943 some 500 P40s armed with the 75/34 gun had been ordered. In September 1943 five pre-series vehicles fell into German hands along with the parts for a further 200.

(*Opposite, below*): The Germans were so impressed by the P26/40 that they built a hundred, although only sixty are thought to have been operational due to engine shortages. A number of P40s without engines were used as static fortifications at Anzio and on the Gustav Line. The Germans had a hundred turrets available for static use, but it is unclear if these were from the completed tanks.

This appears to be a captured Italian M13/40 or M15/42 medium tank, with the German cross just visible on the turret; behind it is possibly an L6/40 light tank. The leaf-sprung suspension in the foreground belongs to a German Maultier cargo half-track. The unit may be the 7th SS Mountain Division.

(*Opposite, top*): AB 43 and AB 41 Italian armoured cars. The Germans seized about sixty Italian armoured cars and had several hundred more built.

(*Opposite, below*): British forces examining captured German assault guns and self-propelled guns; just visible in the background to the left are two Semoventes.

Hitler did not allow the Repubblica Sociale Italiana's armed forces to have any significant numbers of tanks. Just two armoured groups – 'Leoncello' and 'San Giusto', equipped with some M13/40 and M14/41 medium tanks – supported the four divisions of the RSI Army, while the GNR Combattente had a single armoured battalion. The RSI launched an abortive attack on the Allies in December 1944.

Chapter Six

Tanks at Monte Cassino

In an effort to break the disastrous stalemate at Anzio, the Allies launched Operation Diadem on 11 May 1944. The key Allied armoured formations involved in the battle were the US 1st, Canadian 5th and British 6th Armoured Divisions, as well as the Polish 2nd Armoured Brigade. This was an all-out armoured thrust designed to pierce the German defences; it also served to distract Hitler from the impending invasions of Normandy and the French Riviera, and the massive Soviet offensive on the Eastern Front. After months of deadlock the honour of taking Monte Cassino would eventually fall to Polish Shermans.

Operation Diadem called for a rapid penetration of the Gustav Line at Cassino and a joint thrust northwards. Lieutenant General Oliver Leese's British 8th Army was to push up the Liri valley as far as Sora and up the Sacco valley as far as Valmontone, southeast of Rome. Lieutenant General Mark Clark's US 5th Army was to drive along the coast to link up with the US 6th Corps, which would break out from the Anzio beachhead and strengthen the final push on Rome.

On the left two British divisions were to push up the coast to pin down the 3rd Panzergrenadiers, and in the meantime the US 1st Armored and 3rd and 45th Infantry Divisions were to conduct the main attack towards Campoleone. The fighting was heavy, with the Americans losing a hundred tanks, and little progress was made until the 1st Armored Division finally pieced the Caesar Line.

During the fierce battles for Cassino tanks proved to be of limited value; in the town itself they were hampered by rubble and craters which prevented them from moving freely. During the First Battle, when the houses and streets of Cassino were still recognisable, tanks losses were high because they made suicidal frontal assaults and blundered into anti-tank ambushes and well laid mines. In just twelve days of fighting the US 756th Tank Battalion had twenty-three of its sixty-one tanks knocked out, with another twenty-one damaged. An armoured sortie into the Cassino massif early in the Third Battle was hopelessly mismanaged, resulting in considerable losses.

The defenders had no intention of surrendering any ground. During March and April the German paratroopers toiled on Cassino's defences, hauling up their anti-tank guns to protect the most vulnerable sectors, as well as manning the fortified dugouts and bunkers that overlooked the approaches to the top of the Cassino massif. In addition, between Cassino and Rome the Germans had constructed a whole series of defensive lines upon which they could fall back. One of the strongest was the Hitler Line; this was studded with Panther tank turrets embedded in concrete, which were ready to exact an appalling toll on Allied tanks and infantry.

The battle for Monte Cassino comprised four major engagements, involving American, British, Canadian, French, New Zealand and Polish forces. The centrepiece of the battle was the struggle for the monastery overlooking the town of Cassino. By early 1944 the western section of the German Winter Line was held by their forces in the Rapido, Liri and Garigliano valleys, and the surrounding mountains and ridges known as the Gustav Line. The Germans did not occupy the monastery and incorporate it into their defences until after American bombers flattened it in mid-February.

After struggling for six weeks through 7 miles of the Bernhardt Line at the cost of 16,000 casualties, the US 5th Army finally reached the Gustav Line on 15 January. The first assault was launched two days later. Although US troops got across the Rapido, tanks were unable to reach them, leaving them at the mercy of the panzers and self-propelled guns of General Eberhard Rodt's 15th Panzergrenadiers.

When the Third Battle commenced on 15 March it was hoped to launch a decisive blow on the German defences in the monastery and town. This included a surprise attack by the British 20th Armoured Brigade moving up a track from Cairo to Albaneta Farm towards the monastery. The conditions were completely unsuitable for tanks. A German counterattack from the monastery left the tanks stranded round Castle Hill; lacking infantry support, by mid-afternoon they were all knocked out.

The final battle commenced with Operation Diadem on 11 May and saw the British 8th Army make two opposed crossings over the Rapido river. Once this was bridged, tanks of the Canadian 1st Armoured Brigade moved up to support the infantry – armoured support had been lacking during the first two battles. In the meantime the Polish Corps fought against the German paratroops in and around Cassino in what was clearly a grudge match.

While the Polish Corps consisted of two infantry divisions, the 3rd Carpathian and 5th Kresowa, they had the normal allotment of divisional tanks and were supported by the Polish 2nd Armoured Brigade. The latter consisted of the 1st and 2nd Polish and 6th Kresowa Armoured Regiments, equipped with American-supplied Shermans. In total the Poles mustered 50,000 men, who had arrived in Italy between December 1943 and January 1944 and first went into the line in March. Around 80 per cent of these troops were former Russian prisoners of war, but they were strengthened with Poles from the Carpathian Brigade that fought with the

British 8th Army at Tobruk. A Polish armoured division was formed but this was committed to the Normandy campaign.

After the failure of the assaults by the Americans, New Zealanders and Indians, the same formidable defences confronted the Poles. In particular, the monastery, the south and west of the massif, and part of the town were held by the paratroops, whose key strongpoints were situated at Colle Sant' Angelo–Point 706–Monte Castellone; in the monastery and the upper reaches of the town; on Points 593 and 569; and around Massa Albaneta.

The German 1st Parachute Division holding Cassino had considerable firepower. It was supported by 242 Assault Battalion, 525 Anti-tank Battalion (equipped with self-propelled 88mm guns), four artillery battalions from the 10th Army and one from the 90th Panzergrenadier Division. In addition, 71 Werfer Regiment had forty 150 and 300mm mortars near Pignataro and thirty 150mm and 200mm mortars at Villa Santa Lucia. The Nebelwerfer or 'Moaning Minnie' six-barrelled rocket launcher was a particularly devastating weapon.

The Poles had great difficulties in concentrating their men at the forward jump-off points, and were assisted by five Cypriot mule companies and two British jeep platoons in moving up their stockpiles for the attack. The 3rd Carpathians had the job of storming the monastery ruins after securing Point 593 and Albaneta Farm to the northwest. The 5th Kresowas were to assault Phantom Ridge and Sant' Angelo to the south. The going was tough for all the Allied forces committed to the offensive. Astonishingly, within 20 minutes of the opening Allied barrage the Carpathians were on Point 593 and the Kresowas had gained Phantom ridge, though they suffered fearful casualties in the process.

Polish tanks with names like *Claw*, *Pygmy* and *Pirate* advanced on Albaneta on 15 May firing on burnt-out Allied tanks, the remains of the March attack, which were being used as enemy machine-gun posts. They were soon halted by mines, and sappers had to crawl under the tanks for protection from snipers as they worked to clear them. 'We were in utter despair,' said one Polish tank commander, 'being unable to reach our comrades dying in front of Albaneta. With real fury we blasted away at the ruins, and at every suspicious bush or pile of stones.' The tankers took no chances and showed no mercy. Anything that moved was deluged in machine-gun and anti-tank gun fire by the Polish tanks. On the night of 17 May the determined Poles finally gained all their main objectives, including Point 593, but not Albaneta, where the Germans clung on to the last.

Polish troops moved into the monastery on 18 May to find it abandoned. The 1st Parachute Division had called it a day. Lieutenant Casimir Gurbiel and a platoon of Uhlans from the Podolski Lancers were the first Poles to enter the monastery. The only remaining Germans were the badly wounded; when asked why they had held out so fanatically, they replied they had been told the Polish did not take prisoners. Nearly a thousand Poles died in the two attacks.

Six days later the Canadian 5th Armoured Division breached the line, opening the route to Rome. The Allies hoped that this would break the deadlock that had blighted the Italian campaign to date. It was not to be.

The battle for Monte Cassino comprised four major engagements, involving American, British, Canadian, French, New Zealand and Polish forces. This Canadian rifleman, armed with the Lee Enfield No.4 Mk I rifle, was photographed during the fighting against German paratroops at Ortona in late 1943. This was dubbed 'the Italian Stalingrad' such was the ferocity of the combat.

This young German airborne soldier was killed at Ortona on 21 December 1943. The German 1st Parachute Division was one of the key units holding Monte Cassino.

Vehicles from the US 5th Army pushing through the village of Mignano in sight of Cassino. The mountains in the background were in German hands and the village itself came under regular artillery fire.

A New Zealander Sherman on the slopes at Cassino. The fighting around the town and monastery was to turn the area into a tank graveyard.

(*Opposite, top*): The monastery at Monte Cassino after it was hit by Allied bombers. It was first attacked on 15 February 1944 when 576 tons of bombs were dropped on it; the March ground attack was also preceded by an air raid in which 1,140 tons of bombs were delivered by 338 heavy and 176 medium bombers. The rubble in fact aided the defenders, who converted it into a series of strongpoints.

(*Opposite, below*): German paratroops shelter with the crew of an assault gun in the ruins at Cassino. Their StuG III was concealed in the building, in an ideal ambush position.

The German paratroops at Cassino were supported by considerable anti-tank fire power, which included such weapons as this Pak 40 and self-propelled 88mm guns. In addition, between Cassino and Rome lay a whole succession of defensive lines on which they could slowly fall back. One of the toughest in terms of fending off Allied tanks was the Hitler Line (which looped behind the Gustav Line), which was strengthened by Panther tank turrets embedded in concrete.

(*Opposite, top*): Panzertruppen struggling to repair a track on their Panzer Mk IV Ausf H at Monte Cassino.

(*Opposite, below*): A German paratroop mortar team from the 1st Parachute Division. During March and April they strengthened their anti-tank defences by hauling guns to the most vulnerable sectors. The paratroops at Monte Cassino fought bitterly to prevent its capture by a Polish infantry division and armoured brigade.

Men of the 9th Gurkha Rifles moving up a mountain road towards Cassino and Hangman's Hill in mid-March 1944. Like the New Zealanders, they suffered heavy casualties on the slopes below the monastery.

Sherman tanks of the New Zealand 19th Armoured Regiment edging cautiously through the rubble of Cassino; during the battle itself armour was very much relegated to a supporting role. The New Zealand Corps spent two weeks battering their heads against the German defences at Cassino before they were ordered to consolidate their gains.

During the battles for Cassino, tanks proved to be of limited value; in the town itself Allied armour was hampered by rubble and craters that prevented them from moving freely. Albaneta Farm proved to be a particularly devastating killing ground for British and Polish tanks. The first image shows the remains of a New Zealand welded-hull Sherman.

A soldier from the British 8th Army examines the burnt and smashed remains of a Panzer Mk IV Ausf J. It appears to have been caught by Allied bombers, hence the large crater. This tank belonged to the 26th Panzer Division, which fought in the Salerno and Cassino areas from January to May 1944.

The devastated ruins of Cassino town.

(*Opposite, top*): Canadian troops examine a German MG34 machine gun; this, along with the MG42, was the German Army's main squad support weapon. It had a vastly higher rate of fire than the British Bren gun.

(*Opposite, below*): An armoured car and soldiers from the Brazilian 1st Infantry Division in the village of Massarosa. The 25,000-strong Brazilian Expeditionary Force arrived in Italy in August 1944; their first action saw the 6th Combat Team capture Massarosa, north of Lake Massaciuccoli. The Brazilians were the first South American soldiers ever to fight on European soil. They later took part in the US 4th Corps' major assault in April 1945 that pierced the Germans' remaining defences and carried the 5th Army to the Alps.

New Zealanders stand guard over captured German paratroopers gathered by the back of a Sherman.

American gunners taking on ammunition for their self-propelled gun. The capture of Cassino heralded yet more interminable fighting in Italy.

Chapter Seven

Piercing the Gustav Line

The French took credit for the success of Operation Diadem, as it was they who turned the panzers. The French Expeditionary Corps started to arrive in Italy in November 1943 and by May 1944 was fully up to strength. Colonial Moroccan troops first really made their presence felt in Italy when General André Dody's division tipped the balance during Operation Raincoat in mid-December 1943. His men helped push the Germans back to the Gustav Line, but overall the offensive failed to put the Allies in a strong position to support the forthcoming Anzio landings.

While the US 5th Army suggested advancing along the Ausente valley, it was the French General Juin who proposed attacking through the mountains while making no attempt to outflank Aurunci. To do this it was necessary to break out of the Garigliano bridgehead so the French could take Monte Majo and the Ausonia defile. General Clark, impressed by Juin's boldness, agreed.

The 2nd Moroccan Infantry Division under General Dody was given the task of taking Majo and its three spurs. On the right was Brosset's 1st Free French Division and on the left de Monsabert's 3rd Algerian Infantry Division, which was tasked with securing Castleforte to open up the Ausente. Afterwards the Mountain Corps, comprising General Savez's 4th Moroccan Mountain Division and General Guillame's Group of Moroccan Tabors, could then push to the Aurunci massif.

On 13 May 1944, in the face of stiff German resistance, the Moroccans succeeded in breaching the Gustav Line at Monte Majo, one of its deepest (though most weakly defended) points. Ausonia was captured two days later. In particular, the fall of Majo unhinged the 14th Panzer Corps' left wing, greatly contributing to the Allies' success.

By 1730 on 23 May General B.M. Hoffmeister, commanding the Canadian 5th Armoured Division, felt a large enough breach had been achieved to commit his tanks. Unfortunately the division had to shift its axis of attack and got tangled up with the tanks of the 25th Armoured Brigade moving to rearm and refuel. By the time the mess was sorted out too much time had passed and Hoffmeister was unable to attack until early the next morning. This was to become an all-too-familiar problem.

His lead units kicked off at 0800 on 24 May. The vanguard was led by a composite group of tanks and infantry made up of squadrons from the British Columbia Dragoons, each supported by carrier-borne infantry from the Irish Regiment of Canada. This was known as Vokes Force (after the commander of the Dragoons, Lieutenant Colonel F.A. Vokes) and its mission was to establish a base midway between the Hitler Line and Melfa. A second Canadian composite group, Griffin Force, consisting of tanks from Lord Strathcona's Horse (commanded by Lieutenant Colonel P.G. Griffin) and lorried infantry from the Westminster Regiment, was to pass through Vokes Force and take a crossing over the Melfa. A third leap was to be made by elements of the Westminsters who would consolidate the bridgehead, while the 8th Princess Louise's Hussars would fight their way towards Ceprano.

Hoffmeister's tanks were protected on the flanks by the British 6th Armoured Division moving on their right along Highway Six, and by the Canadian 1st Infantry Division on the left, whose tanks and infantry were to strike along the north bank of the Liri. It was during these operations that some of the few major tank-versus-tank battles of the Cassino campaign were fought. It was now that the Allies first came up against the Panzer Mk V Panther in Italy. On 15 May, after urgent appeals from General von Vietinghoff, a company of Panthers had been deployed to Melfa, where they arrived five days later, just in time to confront the Canadians.

Shortly after midday the tanks of the British Columbia Dragoons and supporting infantry reached their objective about 2 miles northwest of Aquino, and Griffin Force was ordered forwards. At 1500 the Strathcona's reconnaissance troop crossed the Melfa. Vokes Force had brushed with the Panthers early on 24 May and remarkably had managed to account for three Panthers for the loss of just four Shermans.

A and C Companies of the Strathconas, trying to cross further north, managed to drive the Panthers to the far bank, but they lost seventeen Shermans and claimed just five panzers destroyed, not all of them Panthers. An infantry officer spoke of the Canadian tank crews with amazement: 'I'll never forget the way the tanks would keep coming and then one would get knocked out and then another and still they'd keep coming.'

Meanwhile the Canadians were unable to get any anti-tank weapons over to the Strathcona/Westminster bridgehead and the Germans launched three counterattacks with Panthers. Three tanks almost overran their positions but PIAT fire made the Germans lose their nerve and they wheeled away. Fortunately by 2100 some 6-pounder anti-tank guns had got over the river.

In summing up the Melfa battles a staff officer in the Canadian 5th Armoured Division wrote:

> As for the main obstacle of the German tanks ... the only reason why it was possible to make headway against their qualitative superiority was by weight of numbers ... General Leese [Commanding 8th Army] was prepared to lose 1,000 tanks. As he had 1,900 at his disposal, the Panther stood a fair chance of becoming an extinct species among the fauna of S. Italy. On our side losses had to be taken and replacements thrown in. Being somewhat up against it, the tankmen were compelled to improvise and make the most of what they had.

It was decided to throw everything up the Liri valley as soon as possible. The net result was that five divisions (Canadian 5th Armoured, British 6th Armoured, Canadian 1st Infantry, Indian 8th Infantry and British 78th Infantry) were all madly jostling for space. This meant that around 450 medium tanks, 240 light tanks, 50 self-propelled guns, 320 armoured cars, 200 scout cars, 2,000 half-tracks and 10,000 lorries were jammed along the roads in the valley. Operation Diadem turned into one enormous traffic jam that threatened to derail the offensive before it had even properly got under way. The military police trying to sort out the chaos were faced with an almost impossible task as tempers flared and vehicles bumped into one another. The slow-moving tanks consumed four times as much petrol as normal and the heavy traffic prevented extra fuel being brought up. It is hardly surprising that the Germans slipped the noose.

On 24 May the British 6th Armoured Division was held up for several hours waiting for the Canadian 5th Armoured Division to clear the roads. On the 29th and 30th, with Acre cleared and 13th Corps thrusting for Altari, an attempt was made to commit yet more tanks, this time the South African 6th Armoured Division. The plan was for the South Africans to replace the Canadians, but until they took over the Canadian positions all they did was add a few more thousand vehicles to the existing almighty traffic jam.

In the meantime the Germans did what they were best at and conducted highly successful local defensive actions. The 90th Panzergrenadiers at Ceprano and the 1st Parachute Division at Acre managed to hold the British at bay and kept the road to Rome closed until the end of May. The Allied command despaired of their tanks ever doing what they were supposed to do.

Meanwhile the German 14th Army conducted an orderly fighting withdrawal towards Rome. Diadem cost the British and American forces some 44,000 casualties, failed to destroy the Germans and condemned the Allies to another year of fighting around the Gothic Line from August 1944 to May 1945. The Germans lost 450 panzers, half the available armour in Italy, as well as 720 guns of various calibres. Four of Kesselring's battered infantry divisions had to be withdrawn for refit and another seven were badly weakened. Nonetheless, four fresh divisions and a regiment of heavy tanks were on the way to help hold up the Allied advance.

The Italian capital was not secured until 4 June, and even then the Allies failed to encircle Kesselring's withdrawing forces. South of Rome the Germans made one last desperate attempt to stop their 10th and 14th Armies losing contact. The diary of an artilleryman serving with the German 65th Infantry Division recalled: 'The whole day Tommy [British troops] is attacking. We answer until the gun barrels are red hot. At 12.15 groups of enemy tanks are trying to break through at the Schotterstrasse [disused railway bed]. This attack collapses in our fire. At 1600 Tommy attacks again. Soon after that we receive orders to retreat.' The 65th Infantry Division destroyed 168 Allied tanks in front of the Schotterstrasse and at Campoleone to the east. Yet still the Allies pressed home their attacks.

Raleigh Trevelyan, a British platoon commander serving with the Green Howards, recalled:

> Sometimes a [Panzer] Mark IV tank or scout car would block main highways into Rome, and partisans would guide the Americans through back alleys. ... At about 8pm Irish Dominicans at San Clemente near the Colosseum heard a commotion like big wheels grinding and went out to investigate. A line of American tanks was drawn up close to the walls of the college. Two of the Fathers walked along the tanks, but no soldier spoke or made a noise. Suddenly from the last tank there jumped an officer, who went down on his knees and asked for a blessing.

The tough Hermann Göring Division, though badly mauled, escaped. Unfortunately for Kesselring, this division was sent to Russia the following month. The British 8th Army struggling up the Adriatic coast by mid-September was being resisted by elements of ten German divisions. This did not greatly deter its advance on the Senio river and by the end of the year the key armoured formations of the German 10th Army, the 26th Panzer and 90th Panzergrenadier Divisions, had suffered ever heavier casualties. Only the arrival of the 29th Panzergrenadier Division alleviated the pressure on the exhausted 26th Panzer and staved off collapse.

This dramatic photo was taken at a US 5th Army forward artillery observation post at Francolise during a 25-pounder barrage on German positions across the Savone river in November 1943. On the west coast the 5th Army had taken Mondragone and the road junction of Sessa Arunca, and by 9 November was approaching the Garigliano.

A disabled Panzer Mk IV captured during the British advance on Villa Grande. This is probably an Ausf G or H. After the taking of Ortona by the British 8th Army on 28 December 1943, troops from the Indian Division occupied positions a quarter of a mile beyond Villa Grande.

A British Honey light tank rounding a bend on its way to the Sangro river from Baglieta, with the Maiella mountains in the background. This photograph was taken on 9 December 1943. In the face of appalling weather conditions and stiff enemy resistance, the British 8th Army carried the river and drove on the port of Pascara.

A column of three Shermans and a carrier come under German mortar fire during the battle of the Sangro river in early December 1943.

Infantry of the Seaforth Highlanders of Canada searching German prisoners near the Moro river on 8 December 1943.

A D8 bulldozer retrieves two Canadian Shermans that came off the road north of San Leonardo di Ortona on 10 December 1943.

German defences in Orsogna under attack by Curtiss P-40 Kittyhawk dive-bombers on 22 December 1943. The British reached Orsogna in early December but the Germans counterattacked and expelled them. The British attacked again, only to discover that the Germans had dug in a Panzer Mk IV and a flamethrower in the town square covered by machine guns positioned in the surrounding houses. This led to heavy street-to-street fighting while the main Allied advance pushed up the east coast towards Pescara.

German gunners score a direct hit on a house in Castel Frentano. The Kittyhawk attack on Orsogna was followed up by thirty-six medium bombers; although the German anti-aircraft defences were weaker than usual, they retaliated by shelling the forward communication road in front of Castel Frentano, a mile from their lines.

General Bert Hoffmeister, commander of the Canadian 5th Armoured Division. His men, in the shape of Vokes Force and Griffin Force, were committed to Operation Diadem on 24 May 1944. Their flanks were protected by the British 6th Armoured Division and the Canadian 1st Infantry Division.

Tanks from the Canadian 5th Armoured Division moving up for the Diadem offensive. Note the carrier stranded in the mud in the lower right of the frame.

Canadian tanks from Vokes Force first came up against the Panzer MK V Panther in the Melfa area on 24 May 1944. The engagement resulted in the loss of four Shermans and three Panthers. Gathering their wits, the panzers subsequently knocked out seventeen Shermans for the loss of just five of their number.

Griffin Force struggled to get its 6-pounder anti-tank guns over the Melfa to fend off German counterattacks with Panthers. Three panzers overran the Canadian positions but the crews lost their nerve and withdrew, by which time help was on its way.

US M10 tank destroyers roll past the Colosseum. American tanks entered Rome on 4 June 1944, to be greeted by Dominican monks.

(*Above and opposite, top*): American M4 Shermans passing through Italian streets. The first photograph depicts an early model M4A1, identifiable by the cast hull and one-piece cast nose. In the second photograph the tank in the foreground is also an M4A1, while the one in the background is an M4A4, again with a cast hull but with the three-piece bolted nose.

(*Opposite, below*): Visible are at least eight British Churchill tanks. After fighting against the Gustav Line, the British 8th Army captured Rimini and established a bridgehead over the Marno on 14 September 1944. This was subjected to fierce German counterattacks.

Upgunned Churchill IVs (NA 75) shelling the Gothic Line. They were converted in Tunisia, North Africa (hence NA) when 120 Churchill IVs were fitted with M3 75mm guns and mantlets salvaged from damaged Shermans. They were the first British tanks to take this calibre gun into action and they proved highly successful in the Sicilian and Italian campaigns.

Two knocked-out Tigers in Italy. The lower image shows the first Tiger knocked out by the New Zealand 18th Armoured Regiment in late July 1944, during the push on Florence.

The Red Army's Major General Vasiliev (*centre*) visiting the US 5th Army on Mount Camino. He was particularly interested in Allied battle methods and weapons.

Chapter Eight

Gothic Horror

Manned by Kesselring's 10th and 14th Armies, the Gothic Line was the last major obstacle between the Allies and the Alps and it proved to be probably the best of all the German defences. The Italian landscape also once more assisted the Germans, for in the valley of the upper Tiber the mountainous backbone of the country twists northwestwards to join the Maritime Alps in Liguria. This forms a huge natural barrier between the flat lands of the northeast and central Italy. After Cassino and Rome fell, the series of delaying battles from Trasimere to Florence had bought the German engineers much-needed time. Unfortunately for the Allies, the French, who were their most experienced and effective mountain troops, were withdrawn to fight in southern France.

As it was the very last line in the series, the Germans had had much greater time to prepare it, not to mention the assistance of 15,000 conscripted Italian labourers. Although the Gothic Line was never finished, it still presented a formidable barrier. The positions included Panther tank turrets set in steel and concrete, bunkers, air raid shelters, gun emplacements, minefields and anti-tank ditches as well as an obstacle zone stretching for 10 miles.

The Germans had done everything conceivable to stop the Allied tanks. Anti-tank defences in depth blocked the approaches to Spezia on the west coast. From Carrara the line passed through the mountains north of Pistoia to the fortifications of the Futa Pass, which included anti-tank ditches and concrete casemates and tank turrets. Eastwards to the Adriatic foothills the defences were concentrated along the Foglia to Pesaro. There deep minefields, a tank ditch, pillboxes and tank turrets protected the coastal belt.

The Allies launched the imaginatively titled Operation Olive in late August 1944 with the 8th Army aiming to break through the sector of the Gothic Line held by General Traugott Herr's 76th Panzer Corps (which did not contain any panzer or panzergrenadier divisions). Traugott's positions were assaulted by the Polish 2nd Corps (which included the Polish 2nd Armoured Brigade), the Canadian 1st Corps (Canadian 5th Armoured Division and the British 21st Tank Brigade) and the British 5th Corps (1st Armoured Division, 7th Armoured Brigade and 25th Tank Brigade). The attack fell into four phases: the advance to the Gothic Line, the penetration of its defences, the battle for the Coriano Ridge and the exploitation of this battle. The reality was that Italy was now very much a secondary theatre of operations, as the battle for Normandy was at its height, and the US 5th Army had lost seven divisions that were sent to take part in Operation Dragoon, the invasion of southern France, at the end of August. The US 5th Army and the British 8th Army had seen their strengths fall dramatically from 249,000 to 153,000 men, leaving them just eighteen divisions with which to overwhelm the fourteen divisions of the German 10th and 14th Armies.

The Germans rushed reinforcements forwards, including the 26th Panzer Division, but this did not stop the Allies breaking through and pouring towards Rimini on the east coast. The Germans, though, did not give up so easily and by 4 September the 29th Panzergrenadiers and two infantry divisions had arrived to bolster the German line, causing a slowing of the Allied advance towards the Gemmano and Coriano Ridges. The fighting here was some of the toughest of the entire Italian campaign. The Coriano Ridge battle between 12 and 19 September 1944 required both the British 1st and Canadian 5th Armoured Divisions to overcome the German defences.

By this stage the Germans had been able to bring in the 90th Panzergrenadier Division and the 20th Luftwaffe Field Division, giving them ten divisions with which to oppose the 8th Army. However, the German defence was overcome and on 21 September the 8th Army took Rimini and was at last in the valley of the River Po.

This advance had been at a terrible cost to both sides: the 8th Army suffered 14,000 casualties and the 76th Panzer Corps lost 16,000. In the British sector during September the Allies lost 250 tanks destroyed by the enemy and a similar number either bogged or broken down. Losses in manpower were such that battalions had to be reduced from four to three companies. Notably the 1st Armoured Division received such a terrible mauling that it virtually ceased to exist and was disbanded on 1 January 1945.

The British soon discovered that the Po valley was not the excellent tank country that they had hoped for. Instead it proved to be a boggy expanse covered in a series of watercourses that greatly suited the Germans' finely honed defensive tactics.

On the left the US 5th Army now included the US 1st, British 6th and South African 6th Armoured Divisions as well as the Canadian 1st Tank Brigade. Facing them was the German 14th Army, which included the 16th SS Panzergrenadier Division. By the end of the first week of September the army reserve, consisting of the 29th Panzergrenadiers and the 26th Panzer Division, had been moved to the Adriatic front. On 18 September the British 6th Armoured Division took the San Godenzo Pass on Route 67 to Forli. A month later the US 5th Army gathered its strength for one last push on Bologna; however, the 29th and 90th Panzergrenadiers helped to put an end to any such ambitions, leaving the 5th Army stranded in the mountains over the winter.

A New Zealand welded-hull Sherman tank pictured during the advance towards the city of Florence on 26 July 1944.

(Above and opposite, top): Two late production models of the Tiger knocked out by the New Zealanders south of Florence. Both have the later all-steel disc road wheels. Inevitably they took a heavy toll on enemy tanks before succumbing to superior numbers.

(Opposite, below): The Gothic Line taking a pounding from a 203mm howitzer during August 1944. The intended speed of the Allies' attack meant that there was no need for a corps level artillery plan, though Operation Olive, launched on 25 August, was supported by twenty-seven squadrons of fighter-bombers and medium bombers.

A Sexton self-propelled gun crawling up a hairpin bend in the Italian mountains. Such dust clouds often attracted the attention of enemy gunners. By 27 August the 46th Division had captured Monte Bartolo, Monte Grosso and Monte Tombola. However, getting the 142nd Tank Regiment into position delayed the push on Ponte Rosso on the River Ventena until 1 September. The Canadians on the right also made excellent progress.

(*Opposite, top*): This vehicle is a Priest Kangaroo. The deployment of the Canadian Ram Kangaroo armoured personnel carrier in northwest Europe in the autumn of 1944 was so successful that the commander of the 8th Army asked for a regiment of tracked APCs for Italy. Between October 1944 and April 1945 a total of 102 M7 Priest self-propelled guns were converted to Kangaroo APCs by removing the gun and mount, the ammunition bins and the plating-in of the hull front. This conversion was also carried out on seventy-five Sherman M4A2 gun tanks. The work was done by 8th Army field workshops.

(*Opposite, below*): Sherman crews of the South African 6th Armoured Division getting rid of spent shell cases after a night blitz in support of the opening stages of the spring offensive.

While this British tank crew replenishes their ammunition stocks, the driver plucks a 'liberated' chicken.

(*Opposite, top*): Further illustrating the multi-national nature of the war in Italy, here an American tank crew is tucking in to a meal beside their Sherman.

(*Opposite, below*): Another Sherman negotiates a snowy mountain road. This is an early production M4: note the three-piece nose casting and vision blocks on the glacis plate. Mines and ambushes were occupational hazards on such roads.

British infantry wearing greatcoats to keep out the Italian winter. As in other theatres of operation, the weather was always a problem.

An American quad anti-aircraft gun mounted in a half-track. By this stage of the war the appearance of the Luftwaffe, or indeed the Italian air force in support of their ground troops, was a very rare occurrence.

Assault guns provided the backbone of the German armoured forces in Italy. The vehicle in the foreground appears to be a StuG III Ausf G with the Saukopf gun mantlet. The height of the superstructure on the vehicles in the background indicates they may be Jagdpanzer IVs, which were issued to the tank-hunter detachments of the panzer divisions from March 1944. They first went into action in Italy with the Hermann Göring Division.

The remains of a Semovente assault gun. A German helmet sits perched on the end of the barrel.

Chapter Nine

Defeat on the Po

Mussolini made one last futile effort at the end of 1944. Carried out largely by Italians, the counterattack was launched in the Senio valley on 26 December. Some of the RSI's remaining tanks may have taken part. The 8th Army, although exhausted and short of ammunition, easily stopped this attack.

On the west coast the Germans launched an attack in the Serchio valley, north of Lucca, and broke through to threaten the US 5th Army's lines of communication with its base at Leghorn. The Germans were blocked with the assistance of a division detached from the British 8th Army. This delayed 5th Army's planned attack towards Bologna and in turn brought the British 8th Army to a halt, because it had to conserve ammunition until the Americans were ready.

The requirements of the crumbling Eastern Front saw the departure of the 16th SS Panzergrenadier Division from Italy in the New Year. Kesselring was appointed Supreme Commander West in March 1945 and replaced in Italy by General von Vietinghoff. German forces on the Italian front amounted to twenty-three divisions, with two others partly formed, and six Italian divisions. The 10th and 14th Armies, holding the left and right flanks respectively, each still had a nominal panzer corps.

By the spring of 1945 neither of the German armies had any reserves, although the battered 29th and 90th Panzergrenadier Divisions remained in von Vietinghoff's Army Group Reserve. These units, plus the 26th Panzer Division, continued to fight tenaciously as they were slowly pushed northwards.

The Allied armoured divisions were involved in one last offensive against the Germans, dubbed Operation Grapeshot. This was launched with the aim of breaking out into the Lombardy plains. The 8th Army element of the attack was called Operation Buckland, and the US 5th Army's contribution was Operation Craftsman.

Preparation for Grapeshot commenced on 6 April 1945 when the Germans' Senio defences were subjected to heavy artillery bombardment. Three days later 825 heavy bombers attacked fixed positions beyond the Senio river; these were then followed by medium bombers and fighter-bombers. The latter struck at anything that moved, especially exposed armoured fighting vehicles and motor transport. The air attacks heralded the ground assault against the shell-shocked defenders, which rolled forwards at dusk that day. In support of the New Zealand 2nd Infantry Division were twenty-eight Churchill Crocodile flamethrowers and 127 Carrier Wasp flamethrowers. These scorched everything in their path and by nightfall of 10 April the New Zealanders had reached the Santerno, which they crossed the following day.

The American assault, also preceded by a massive bombardment of enemy positions by heavy bombers and artillery, opened on 14 April with the US 1st Armored Division supporting the US 4th Corps. The following night the US 2nd Corps, which included the South African 6th Armoured Division, attacked towards Bologna between Highways 64 and 65.

The 8th Army had forced the Argenta Gap by 19 April and the British 6th Armoured Division swung left to drive northwestwards along the Reno river to Bondeno, link up with the US 5th Army and encircle the Germans defending Bologna. Bondeno fell on 23 April and the 6th Armoured duly linked up with the Americans at Finale to the north the following day.

Despite Hitler's instructions to stand fast, the Germans had no option but to fall back beyond the River Po. They finally sustained a deathblow trying to escape across the river, losing eighty tanks, 1,000 motor vehicles and 300 pieces of artillery. By this stage continuing the fight in Italy had become pointless. The official unconditional surrender in Italy was signed on 2 May 1945. The remaining panzers and Italian tanks were turned over to the Allies. The Italian campaign was over.

The Allies' 1945 spring offensive included the deployment of twenty-eight Churchill Crocodile flamethrowers (seen here) and 127 Carrier Wasp flamethrowers in support of the New Zealand 2nd Infantry Division. These weapons were devastating against enemy pillboxes and bunkers.

Judging from the fuel trailer, this is another Churchill Crocodile flamethrower, photographed near the Senio river on 9 April 1945.

(*Opposite, top*): A Sherman tank passing a wrecked Tiger on the Senio river on 10 April 1945. New Zealand infantry knocked out the Tiger using a PIAT anti-tank weapon at very close range!

(*Opposite, below*): Another knocked-out panzer, this time a Panther destroyed by the New Zealand 2nd Infantry Division during the attack on the Sillaro river in mid-April 1945.

British stretcher-bearers passing M4A4 Shermans in the town of Portomaggiore, north of Argenta and between Lake Comacchi and Route 16. It was captured by the 8th Army on 19 April 1945. Over 1,600 M4A4s were supplied to the 8th Army in Italy in 1943, and in total 7,499 examples were produced during the war. It was known as the Sherman V to the British Army.

(*Above and opposite, top*): Although work to develop a new light tank to replace the M3 and M5 started in March 1943, the M24 Chaffee was not standardised until mid-1944. The second photograph shows a Chaffee of the US 1st Armored Division on the streets of Milan in late April 1945.

(*Opposite, below*): To the south of Milan the Brazilian Division accepted the surrender of the commander of the 148th Infantry Division, General Otto Fretter-Pico, on 28 April 1945.

Pastore

General Mark Clark, commander of 15th Army Group, takes the surrender of Lieutenant General von Senger und Etterlin, commander of the 14th Panzer Corps, who was representing the German Commander-in-Chief SouthWest, Colonel General von Vietinghoff, on 4 May 1945. Some 230,000 German troops in Italy and southern Austria laid down their arms, finally bringing the fighting in the Italian campaign to a close.

(*Opposite, top*): Abandoned German armoured fighting vehicles and transport vehicles on the road between Finale Emilia and Ferrara. Note the discarded Italian Semovente on the left.

(*Opposite, below*): German troops, having laid down their arms, march into captivity.

A soldier surveys the destruction wrought by the Italian campaign.